POLAR ICE CAPS IN DANGER
EXPEDITION TO ANTARCTICA

John Nelson

PowerKiDS press™

New York

Published in 2009 by The Rosen Publishing Group, Inc.
29 East 21st Street, New York, NY 10010

First Edition

Editors: Joanne Randolph and Gheeta Sobha
Book Design: Greg Tucker
Illustrations: Dheeraj Verma/Edge Entertainment

Library of Congress Cataloging-in-Publication Data

Nelson, John.
  Polar ice caps in danger : expedition to Antarctica / John Nelson. — 1st ed.
      p. cm. — (Jr. graphic environmental dangers)
  Includes index.
  ISBN 978-1-4042-4227-2 (library binding) — ISBN 978-1-4042-4594-5 (pbk.) —
ISBN 978-1-4042-3979-1 (6-pack)
  1. Ice caps—Antarctica—Juvenile literature. 2. Global warming—Juvenile literature.
3. Sea level—Juvenile literature. I. Title.
  GB2597.Y66 2009
  363.738'74—dc22
                                                2007049649

Manufactured in the United States of America

CONTENTS

INTRODUCTION

There are many science centers in Antarctica, the icy continent around the South Pole. By studying Antarctica, scientists have found that **glaciers** began forming about 38 million years ago. Scientists have also discovered that the ice caps covering the South Pole are beginning to melt.

Scientists are concerned about the effects of a large-scale meltdown of the ice caps at both the North and South Poles. What might happen if such a terrible event occurred? Join our expedition to Antarctica to find out.

POLAR ICE CAPS IN DANGER
EXPEDITION TO ANTARCTICA

ANTARCTICA IS THE COLDEST CONTINENT ON EARTH. THE **GLACIAL** WINTER **TEMPERATURES** RUN BETWEEN -121° F (-85° C) AND -130° F (-90° C).

THIS IS THE HOME OF MCMURDO STATION, ANTARCTICA'S LARGEST COMMUNITY AND A FUNCTIONING MODERN SCIENCE CENTER.

THE STATION INCLUDES A HARBOR, THREE AIRFIELDS, A **HELIPORT**, MORE THAN 100 BUILDINGS, A BOWLING ALLEY, AND EVEN A NINE-HOLE GOLF COURSE!

IT IS THE CENTER OF ALL AMERICAN ACTIVITY ON ANTARCTICA. ANYTHING, AND ANYONE, GOING TO THE SOUTH POLE MUST FIRST PASS THROUGH McMURDO.

PROFESSORS HARRIET ADAMS AND RALPH ATKINSON OF McMURDO'S CRARY SCIENCE AND ENGINEERING CENTER GET READY FOR A TRIP.

I HOPE EVERYONE IS READY. WE LEAVE AS SOON AS THE C-130 IS LOADED.

AND THEN IT'S OFF TO THE AMUNDSEN-SCOTT SOUTH POLE STATION, ABOUT THREE HOURS AWAY.

AJAY SINGH AND RACHEL LIU ARE COLLEGE STUDENTS WHO ARE STUDYING WITH THE PROFESSORS.

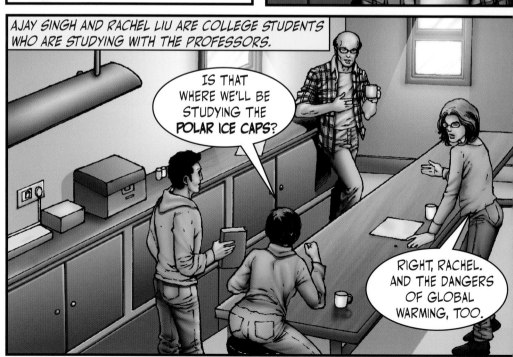

IS THAT WHERE WE'LL BE STUDYING THE **POLAR ICE CAPS?**

RIGHT, RACHEL. AND THE DANGERS OF GLOBAL WARMING, TOO.

I'M PLANNING TO TELL EVERYONE ABOUT SOME OF MY STUDIES WHEN WE GET TO AMUNDSEN-SCOTT.

LET'S GET READY TO MOVE OUT. TAKE EVERYTHING YOU NEED, AND REMEMBER, DRESS WARMLY!

THREE HOURS AND 850 MILES (1,368 KM) LATER, THE TEAM REACHES THE AMUNDSEN-SCOTT STATION.

WOW! WE'RE AT THE VERY TIP OF THE SOUTHERN END OF PLANET EARTH, THE SOUTH POLE!

BUCKLE UP, EVERYONE. WE'RE ABOUT TO LAND!

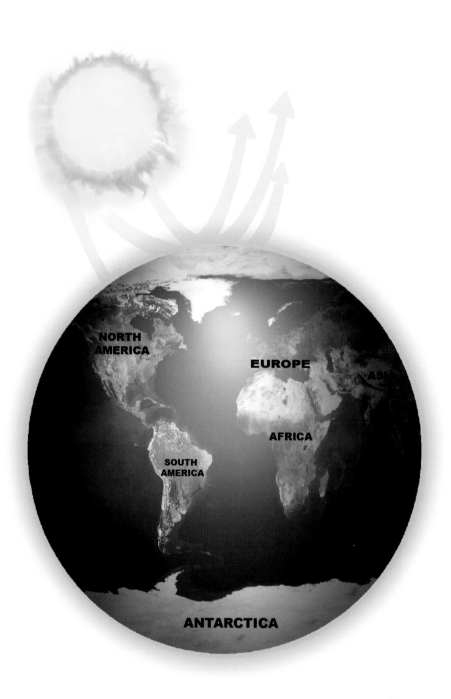

"AN INCREASE OF GREENHOUSE GASES LEADS TO A RISE IN EARTH'S TEMPERATURES.

"THIS HAPPENS WHEN WE BURN FOSSIL FUELS, SUCH AS OIL OR COAL, TO RUN OUR CARS, HEAT WATER, OR MAKE ELECTRICITY."

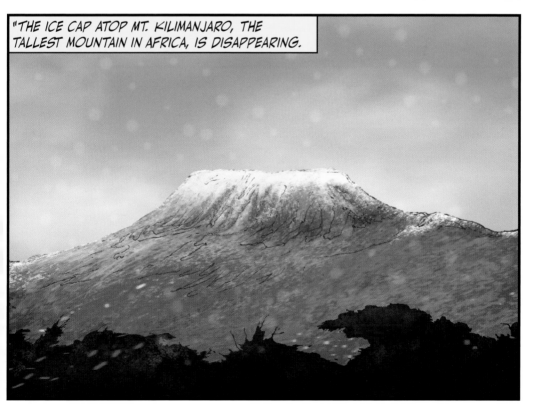

"EVEN GLACIERS IN MONTANA'S GLACIER NATIONAL PARK ARE MELTING MORE EACH YEAR.

"SOME FISH HAVE TROUBLE BREEDING BECAUSE THE OCEAN TEMPERATURE IS RISING.

"SOME ANIMALS ARE HAVING FEWER BABIES BECAUSE CHANGING WEATHER PATTERNS ARE DISRUPTING THEIR MATING SEASONS."

"PEOPLE COULD LOSE THEIR HOMES. WHERE WOULD THEY GO?"

"IN SOME AREAS, FLOODING HAS PUSHED SALT WATER ONTO FARMLAND. THE SALT MAKES THE LAND UNUSABLE FOR GROWING CROPS."

"SOME **EXPERTS** SAY THAT IF THE WORST **PREDICTIONS** COME TRUE, SEA LEVELS COULD RISE 30 FEET (9 M).

"IF SUCH TEMPERATURE CHANGES CONTINUE, THE STATE OF FLORIDA WILL BE TOTALLY UNDER WATER IN 1,000 YEARS!"

ISN'T THERE ANYTHING WE CAN DO TO HELP STOP GLOBAL WARMING, PROFESSOR?

THERE SURE IS, RACHEL. OUR SMALL ACTIONS CAN MAKE A BIG DIFFERENCE.

"YOU CAN START BY PLANTING A TREE!

"TREES TAKE IN THE CARBON DIOXIDE THAT CONTRIBUTES TO GLOBAL WARMING. THEY CHANGE IT INTO OXYGEN AND PUT THE OXYGEN BACK INTO THE AIR.

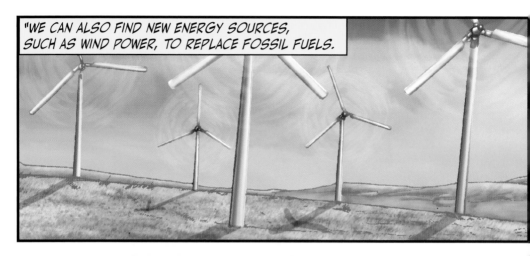

"WE CAN ALSO FIND NEW ENERGY SOURCES, SUCH AS WIND POWER, TO REPLACE FOSSIL FUELS.

"SOLAR POWER IS ANOTHER WAY TO GO, ALTHOUGH IT'S STILL A VERY EXPENSIVE TYPE OF ENERGY TO USE.

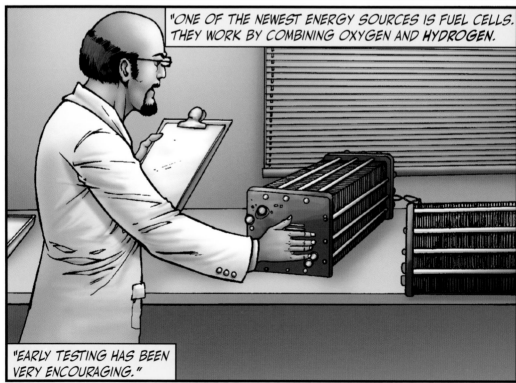

"ONE OF THE NEWEST ENERGY SOURCES IS FUEL CELLS. THEY WORK BY COMBINING OXYGEN AND *HYDROGEN*.

"EARLY TESTING HAS BEEN VERY ENCOURAGING."

SMALL ACTIONS HELP, TOO. DON'T WASTE WATER AND ENERGY.

RECYCLING ALSO HELPS! THE LESS WASTE WE MAKE, THE LESS ENERGY WE NEED TO MAKE NEW PRODUCTS.

BY DOING JUST A FEW SIMPLE THINGS, WE CAN KEEP OUR PLANET HEALTHY.

AND PREVENT OUR POLAR ICE CAPS FROM MELTING!

LAST ONE BACK TO THE SNOWCAT BUYS DINNER!

THE END

FACTS ABOUT ANTARCTICA AND THE POLAR ICE CAPS

1. Antarctica's largest land animal is a midge that is only ½ inch (1.3 cm) long.

2. The lowest recorded temperature on Earth, -128.6° F (-89.2° C), was at Vostok Station on July 21, 1983.

3. There are polar ice caps located in the Arctic area at the North Pole as well as the South Pole.

4. If the ice covering Antarctica melted, the oceans would rise about 200 feet (60 m).

5. A growing hole in the ozone layer over Antarctica, which was caused by pollution, concerns many scientists around the world.

6. Science stations at Antarctica ship wastes back to their home countries to avoid polluting the land.

7. The Antarctic Treaty is an international agreement to treat Antarctica as a peaceful science research area.

8. Antarctica is the driest continent, even though it has the most freshwater, in the form of ice.

9. The ice caps have covered most of Antarctica for about five million years.

10. During the winter months, the sea around Antarctica turns to ice, increasing the continent's size from 7 million square miles (18 million sq km) to 13 million square miles (34 million sq km).

GLOSSARY

DISEASE *(dih-ZEEZ)* An illness or sickness.

DISRUPTING *(dis-RUPT-ing)* Throwing into disorder.

EXPERTS *(EK-sperts)* People who know a lot about a subject.

FILTERING *(FIL-tur-ing)* Flowing through something very slowly to remove unwanted things.

GLACIAL *(GLAY-shul)* Having to do with glaciers and being very cold.

GLACIERS *(GLAY-shurz)* Large masses of ice that move down a mountain or along a valley.

HELIPORT *(HEH-luh-port)* A place where helicopters can land.

HYDROGEN *(HY-dreh-jen)* A colorless gas that burns easily and weighs less than any other known element.

POLAR ICE CAPS *(POH-lur EYES KAPS)* Huge layers of ice and snow that cover large areas of land in the North Pole and South Pole.

PREDICTIONS *(prih-DIK-shunz)* Guesses based on facts or knowledge.

TEMPERATURES *(TEM-pur-cherz)* How hot or cold things are.

THRIVE *(THRYV)* To be successful, to do well.

INDEX

WEB SITES

Due to the changing nature of Internet links, PowerKids Press
has developed an online list of Web sites related to the
subject of this book. This site is updated regularly. Please use
this link to access the list:

www.powerkidslinks.com/ged/polar/